*Analysis of ceramic panel from Sheikh Lotfullah mosque, Isfahan, by Simon Trethewey.
The central medallion is a third of the width of the square. Two systems of spirals, major and
minor, are shown separated top right and combined in the final design.*

Published by
Bloomsbury USA, New York

All papers used by Bloomsbury USA are natural, recyclable
products made from wood grown in well-managed forests.
The manufacturing processes conform to the environmental
regulations of the country of origin.

Library of Congress Cataloging-in-Publication Data
has been applied for.

ISBN-13: 978-1-62040-258-0

First U.S. edition 2013

1 3 5 7 9 10 8 6 4 2

Designed and typeset by
Wooden Books Ltd, Glastonbury, UK

Printed in the U.S.A. by Worzalla,
Stevens Point, Wisconsin

CURVES

FLOWERS, FOLIATES & FLOURISHES
IN THE FORMAL DECORATIVE ARTS

Lisa DeLong

BLOOMSBURY
NEW YORK · LONDON · NEW DELHI · SYDNEY

This effort is indebted to the contributions of Simon Trethewey, John Martineau, and Stephen Parsons. Discussions with Ramiz Sabbagh have also been incredibly useful. Thanks to Ann Hechle for the calligraphy on page 47. This project could not have been conceived without twelve years of association with my colleagues at the Visual Islamic and Traditional Arts department at the Prince's School of Traditional Arts in London, especially Keith Critchlow, Paul Marchant, and Delfina Bottesini. Special thanks to the DeLongs: Dave, Julie, Sarah, Rick, Pete, and Angie. Further sources: Pattern Design *by Lewis Day;* Ornament *by Stuart Durant;* Simple Calyx Ornament in Islamic Art *by F. Shafi'i;* The Grammar of Ornament *by Owen Jones;* Crystal and Dragon *by David Wade;* The Language of Ornament *by J. Trilling.*

Above: Iznik dish decorated with an arrangement of leafed spirals composed with three-fold symmetry in the outer band and seven-fold symmetry in the central medallion. An example of the "rumi" style of leafy ornament, with teardrop-shaped leaves composed of smaller leaves whose placement is structured by a framework of nested hexagons and triangles.

CONTENTS

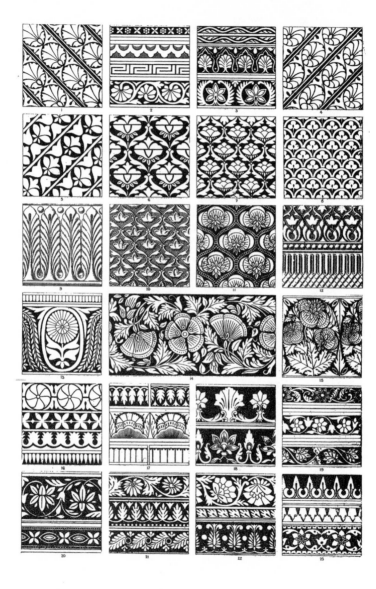

INTRODUCTION

The urge to adorn and beautify sacred things and ordinary objects is universal. Ancient myths worldwide hint at Nature's symbolism and ornamental significance. Trees of Life, leafy crowns, richly decorated robes, and even palaces and temples echo her fertile forms. In each case, the application of symbolic ornament endows an object with both aesthetic and metaphysical value. Our instinct to decorate is ancient.

Nature is complex. She is elegant and serene, turbulent and wild. Her forms can be beautiful, graceful, vicious, brutal, or delicate—but they are always fit for purpose. Owen Jones, author of *The Grammar of Ornament*, who drew the plate of Indian ornament opposite, wrote of Nature: "See how various the forms, and how unvarying the principles." These principles of generation, growth, symmetry, and order also govern the curvilinear ornamentation found in the art of every culture.

Principles do not constrain creativity; rather they inspire diverse and imaginative echoes of seeds, vines, leaves, flowers, and fruit. A designer who works with repetition, alternation, undulation, tesselation, spirals, and symmetry soon discovers the rich variety made possible by working with these simple generative processes. The designs opposite incorporate these principles in their microcosmic gardens of paradise, giving a glimpse of the abundant liveliness of curvilinear decoration found across the globe. It is hoped that readers will discover their own sources of inspiration in the echoes of Nature and the principles of design gathered here.

EARLY CURVES
primordial patterns

Ornament brings cosmology into our mundane world. What may initially appear to be superficial decoration can in fact represent transformational principles and deep structural insights. Ananda Coomaraswamy writes that "the human value of anything made is determined by the coincidence in it of beauty and utility."

The earliest surviving prehistoric clay vessels (*e.g. opposite*) embody this creative urge to participate in the transfiguration of the ordinary. Formless clay was centered on a wheel and spiralled upward in a potter's hands as it was shaped into a vessel. The meanings of the painted spirals, loops, folds, and clefts are lost to time, but the modern eye sees profound beauty in the lines of energy and flow.

The human desire to decorate knows no bounds. Traditional oceangoing Pacific cultures such as the Maori often decorated their entire bodies with tattoos, including their faces, using the same swirling patterns seen on their paddles and canoes (*see below*).

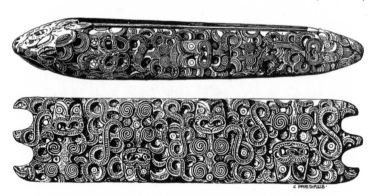

Jiangxi Prov., China, 8,000 BC

Yangshao Culture, China, 4,000 BC

Majiayao Culture, China, 3,000 BC

Machiayao Culture, China, 3,500 BC

Trypillian Culture, Romania, 4,000 BC

IN THE BEGINNING
point, separation, and reunification

The visual richness and complexity of biomorphic ornament often obscures the underlying principles of its design. A core matrix of simple forms regularly hides beneath the leaves and flowers.

A point origin • is the microcosmic germ of life, expressed macrocosmically as a circle ○. The point slides to create a line ⌐, rotation yields a circle ↻, the circle stretches into a drop shape ◌, the drop spins to introduce a form found in both the positive and negative spaces of many curved designs ℓ, and circles overlap to produce leaves and petals 0.

Separation, convergence, and reunification recur as lines spring from points of generation, branch, flower, and return. C- and S-shaped curves are especially useful elements for building a compositional structure (*opposite*). The proportions can be stretched and squashed, drawn freehand, or geometrically regulated. Below are examples of curves from square and hexagonal circle grids— useful "spines" for linear compositions and border designs.

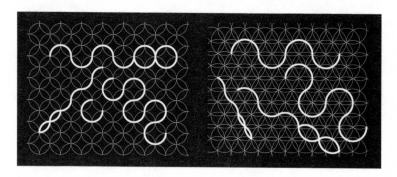

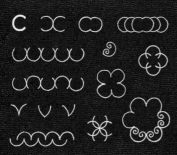

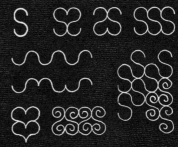

Above: The C-shape and its family.

Above: The S-shape and its designs.

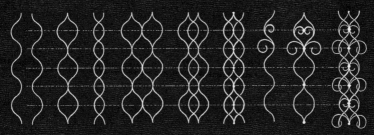

Above and below: The evolution of a simple biomorphic element, showing the layers and essential rhythms.

STRUCTURE AND MOVEMENT
line and curve

Geometrical grids are highly useful to designers. They provide a formal linear trellis for curves to cling to and spring from, a structured counterpoise to curvilinear movement, growth, and fertile development. Straight-edged patterns with sharp corners can evolve into waves and ripples, whilst the softening of corners and edges can transfigure crystals into flowers and transpose staccato rhythms into melodic compositions.

Geometrical designs display strong visual repeats, from chessboard grids to simple brickwork and basic weaving patterns. However, many often have a lifeless quality, and it is only when the straight lines of the grids are brought to life like spreading ripples on a lake or the oscillating strings of a violin that they begin to pulse and transform toward the living forms of biomorphic designs.

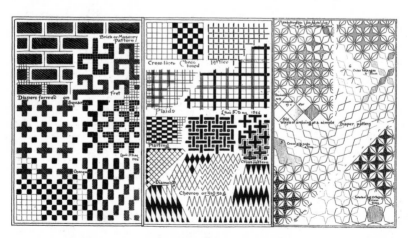

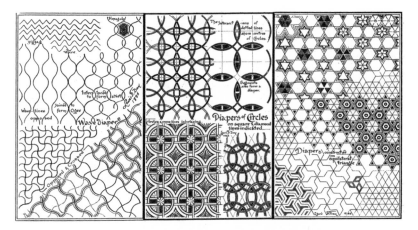

This page and opposite: Known as "diaper" patterns, these playful explorations of geometric and curvilinear pattern by Lewis F. Day (1898) offer a small glimpse of the design possibilities across the plane. Notice how curvilinear designs emerge from straight line grids. These examples are based on the three simple regular tilings: squares, triangles, and hexagons. However, other novel and intriguing possibilities quickly appear once semi-regular structures are employed, for example octagonal, rectangular, or rhomboid grids.

YIN AND YANG
opposition and complementarity

Curved forms embody the principle of "give and take"—as one edge advances, another recedes. This relationship is beautifully illustrated in the "yin-yang" motif which expresses the interdependence of opposites: female and male, black and white, active and receptive, manifest and mysterious. Each principle is incomplete without its partner; each is found at its partner's core.

In any design, positive and negative space are bound together as parts of a whole, mutually defining one other. A successful design often demands that the "negative" background space that is *not*, be as beautiful as the "positive" foreground space that *is*.

The single "teardrop" shape itself is ubiquitous, and may manifest as a paisley (*see pages 50–51*), a single leaf or young flower bud, the open spaces of Gothic tracery (*lower, opposite*), or gilded rumi motif leaves twining around the margins of an illuminated Turkish Quran.

In the 19th-century Azeri jewelry piece shown below, spirals and teardrops are playfully combined.

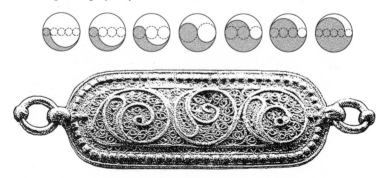

Above: A rumi motif is similar to the paisley or yin-yang shape, here shown with fractal infill.

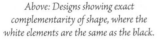

Above: Designs showing exact complementarity of shape, where the white elements are the same as the black.

Below and right: A significant element of Gothic tracery is the graceful, tapering yin-yang shape. These playful German compositions illustrate just how flexible a system based on these forms can become.

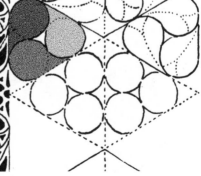

ELEMENTS
action, reaction, and interaction

Natural forces appear everywhere in the decorative arts—watery spirals, shoots forcing up through the earth to unfurl leaves, blossoms opening petals to the radiant sun; biomorphic decoration reflects Nature's fierceness, cyclical rhythms, and transformative power.

The freedom of movement found in curvaceous ornamentation is an interpretation of the order of Nature and her elemental principles and symmetries. Many cultures evolve designs which attempt to convey these often abstract and fluid concepts.

In Japanese art, echoing nature, designs depict the flow form interactions of elements over time—ripples in wet sand, eddies in a stream, arched rocks sculpted by wind, streams of molten lava, crack patterns, cloud formations, and crossing branches.

This page and opposite: In these classical Japanese textile designs (after Jeanne Allen), elemental forces combine and coalesce as blossoms drifting down a stream, metal shattering the air, radiant flame, windblown clouds, eddies of water, and bamboo thrusting upward from the earth. Each design is a piece of art which, in the words of Thomas Aquinas "imitates Nature in the manner of her operation."

SEEDS AND ORIGINS
the mystery of life

Life begins with a seed that swells, sprouts, and begins to grow, a process echoed in biomorphic ornamentation. The designer first establishes a point of origin from which all stems and branches spring. These then serve as generation points for more vines, branches, leaves, and flowers. Ultimately, each part of the composition is traceable to one source and maintains a consistent direction of growth.

The artist may choose to reveal the point of origin as a seed or a cluster of roots. In many cases, however, the mystery of the origin is hidden from direct view behind a veil of clouds, a knot or medallion, or concealed within a vase (*see Indian fabric, Iznik plate, and Persian wall tiling, opposite*). Any change in the direction of growth would break the continuity and logic of the design. In the rare cases when this becomes necessary, the designer obscures these inflection points in some way by a flower, a ring or knot, or some other sign that suggests a new node of origin.

The shape within which a composition grows needs to be handled sensitively, the artist responding to it with well-balanced, space-filling foliates (*as illustrated in the Mughal box lid, below*).

SPIRAL MANIA
vines and spines

Pure spirals are ornaments in their own right, but they can also become the basis of structures from which leaves grow and flowers blossom. Glide, rotation, and reflection symmetries are used by designers to create borders or other ornamentations (*see below*).

A linear sequence of spirals can form a spine from which leaves and flowers may later sprout. Care should be taken to ensure that the spirals spring from one another smoothly and consistently. If floral and foliate elements are to be added, consider how they will respond to the spiral structure.

Tessellated spirals produce lively compositions, while radial arrangements can become the basis of complex rosettes. By changing the type of spiral employed, designs can take on quite different appearances. Examples of various kinds of mathematical spirals are shown in Appendix 1 (*pages 54–55*).

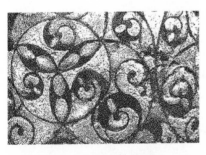

Above left: Egyptian spirals, 2,000 BC with lotus motifs in a variety of compositions (after Glazier). Above right: Late Italian Renaissance stone spiral flourish. Below: Late Roman copper alloy with champlevé enamel vase, central France, 250–300 AD; Celtic spiral design from the 7th c. Book of Durrow; Modern handprinted Indian textile; Detail of Yuan dynasty vase (1,300–50 AD), Jiangxi province, China.

15

IRONWORK
decorative and protective

Ironwork provides an exceptionally clear example of how simple curved elements can be combined into complex ornamentational objects. A quick glance at the examples below and opposite will show that **C** and **S** curves, combined with spirals and a few straight lines, constitute the primary visual vocabulary here.

The first people to smelt and purify iron were the Hittites, around 2,000 BC, but it was not until 17th-century France and Spain that form and function first truly met and the family of iron flourishes was explored. Blacksmiths forged together clusters of **C**- and **S**-shaped spirals to provide both security and beauty in the form of elaborate gates and grills. Needing to find a balance of strength and delicacy, they chose curves which were neither too tight nor too lax and openings not so large that they offered no security nor so tight that they blocked visibility.

The medieval hinges of vast wooden cathedral doors are another wonderful example of the use of iron (*e.g. the hinge from the Cathedral of Notre-Dame, opposite lower left*). In fine detail they often depict trees, evoking the Tree of Life, or Knowledge, thus designating the consecrated space within the church walls as paradisiacal Eden.

Above: A regal set of wrought iron gates from the 19th-century catalogue of the French Denonvilliers company. Notice the various motifs: spirals, C-shapes, S-shapes, and hearts. Below left: Medieval door hinge from the Cathedral of Notre-Dame, Paris. Below right and opposite page: More French wrought ironwork, fences, grills, brackets, and garden lunettes, all using the same simple elements.

LEARNING FROM LEAVES
structure and stylization

A leaf a wondrous thing; it transforms light into nutrients for life. Each leaf, whilst essentially a repetition of every other leaf on a plant, is also completely unique, its veining often suggesting a microcosmic version of the whole of which it is a part.

Leaves come in many shapes and sizes, but the primary distinction is between simple leaves (e.g. aristate 🍃, ovate 🍃, or obcordate 🍃) and compound forms (e.g. palmate 🍃, pinnate 🍃). There can also be different edges to a leaf (e.g. spiny 🍃, serrated 🍃, or lobed 🍃), and there are various veining patterns. For the designer, learning to notice, study, and then stylize Nature's profound and varied forms requires a sensitivity to lines, curves, shapes, universal qualities, and individual quirks.

A widely-used leaf in the classical world was that of the acanthus plant, and it offers a case study of stylization principles in foliate ornamentation. Stylization can take many forms, but each of the iterations shown here (*below and opposite*) retains the essential character of the acanthus.

Stylization is a key part of successful biomorphic design. Other motifs throughout this book provide examples of the principle: the essence of form and energy of growth remain, whilst details are flattened, distilled, and organized to show an ideal form.

This page and opposite: The acanthus leaf has been an important motif since classical times and provides an example of how nature can be stylized. The characteristic principles and energy of its form can be turned into a scrolling border (opposite, two variations of one design), a 2nd-century Roman Corinthian capital (above), other variants (above), or a William Morris pattern (below).

ARABESQUES
a garden around every corner

The "arabesque" is a term used to describe interlaced foliate designs from Islamic art which later permeated the European Renaissance. C-curves, S-shapes, spirals, and undulations are choreographed to produce swooping, flowing, playful adornment for every surface. In these 1856 plates by Owen Jones, regulation and rhythm counterpoints and structures the riot of growth. Look for repetition, alternation, spirals, mirroring, rotation, glides, and the partnering of complementary opposites.

PLANS AND ELEVATIONS
looking at plants from different angles

In biomorphic ornament, plants and plant elements are typically shown either in plan (*from the top, e.g. below*) or in elevation (*from the side, e.g. opposite, top left*), rather than in perspective as in other arts.

The simplest form of elevation appears in palmettes (leaves or petals springing out from a generation point), often seen in Greek ornament. Calyx ornament employs another form of elevation (*see Appendix III, page 58*). Rosettes, meanwhile, are plan-projected flowers with petals or leaves radiating out from a center.

In some instances a fusion may be successfully employed, with the plant rising in elevation and the flowers shown in plan, emerging toward the viewer. Flowers are often stylized to show the eternal essence of flowerness, rather than an individual bloom.

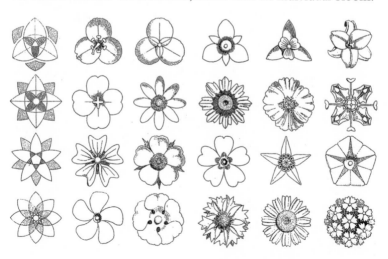

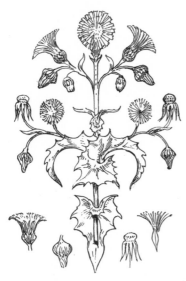

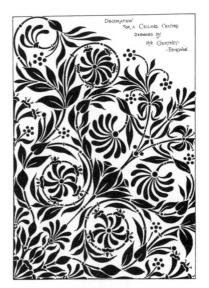

Above: Botanical illustrations need to show a lot of information about a plant, so often show flattened plants in both plan and elevation. Above right: Quarter of a Victorian elevational composition. Below left: Islimi flowers in elevation. Below right: Greek vase with elements in elevation. Opposite: Flowers in plan.

CENTERED COMPOSITIONS
the bee's-eye view

Medallions and rosettes find their way into most floriate decoration. From the grandeur of a cathedral's rose window to a biscuit or a child's shirt button, these motifs bloom everywhere.

Compositions of this form are typically radially symmetric, often combining both rotational and reflective symmetry (*as in the carved stone bosses, below*). Some simply show a flower, while others are a complex arrangement of foliated spirals and curves interspersed with palmettes and calyx ornament (*opposite*).

Many designs appear surprisingly simple once their basic unit is identified, although the artisan must always ensure that the parts all come together in a beautiful whole. Experiment with some tracing paper, rotating and reflecting a design drawn in one-eighth of a circle. Notice too how the vines and leaves of elevation-style motifs, when arranged in a rosette, can unite to create the illusion of a blossom unfolding, petal by petal.

PLANNING WITH GEOMETRY
foreground and background

When ornament adapts to inhabit a shape, the structuring form should contain rather than confine. It is thus often useful when preparing an area for ornamentation to use a proportional system to govern areas of emphasis and the arrangement of major shapes. Although smaller shapes may be intuitively in-filled with flourishes and scrolling ornament, more often the designer will again use an underlying structure (*see examples below*).

An appropriate balance should exist between foreground and background to allow the emptiness of the negative spaces to play a role at least as important as the positive. Designs are made more or less elaborate depending on factors such as the medium, intended use of the decorated object, viewing distance, scale, and style.

Above: The same essential triangular design with different levels of elaboration.

Iznik design from an Ottoman table (1560 AD), ordered by a hexy nest of sixfold stars. Islamic artisans were particularly skilled in structuring their designs, always striving for a balance between order and freedom.

EXTRAVAGANT ORNAMENT
the baby and the bathwater

In the 1600s, an exaggerated form of ornamentation became fashionable in Europe. The new style, known as the Baroque, was driven by a desire for elaborate and grandiose opulence, characterized by increasingly extravagant and floridly flamboyant forms, culminating in the almost cartoonlike 18th-century French Rococo style. Over this period ornamentation became bigger, more asymmetrical and voluptuously curvaceous. Huge cornucopias, shells, nymphs, scrolls, and neopagan and oriental fancies competed for space with old-fashioned foliate themes in houses, gardens (*opposite top*), furniture (*see title page*), and everything else from picture frames to bathtubs, shoes, and fountains. In this period obsessed with flights of fancy and the impossibly bizarre, the seed principle (*page 12*) faded in importance.

As popular revolutions spread across Europe, the Baroque and Rococo styles eventually withered to be replaced by an austere classicism. Today, we live in a world dominated by unornamented rectangles, squares, and straight lines, although gilded encrustations are still a signifier of wealth and decadence.

28

Above: 18th-century Rococo ornament is based on the curves of seashells and parchment scrolls.
Below: Elizabethan strapwork balances positive and negative space. Although both styles often feature
foliate elements, neither generally obeys the traditional "seed" principle (see page 12).

TILES
slide, drop, and rotation

A tile unit need not be elaborate or complicated to produce an interesting pattern. For some tiles, a simple slide may be the only action required to generate a sophisticated design.

In the same way, merely rotating a tile can generate surprisingly complex designs. Tiles intended for rotation usually involve careful consideration of diagonal movement since each 90° twist brings a new corner into play. Consider the examples shown (*opposite*): some motifs on the edges and corners are halved or quartered because they extend past the limits of the tile. When the tile is tessellated, these motifs are made whole. The "missing" portions are cleverly designed to be completed by rotation, reflection, and glide.

A *drop pattern* is one in which the design is planned in such a way that the basic unit repeats when slid down by a set proportion, most commonly by one half its height. This type of repeat is typically used in wallpapers, since it allows horizontal seams to be offset (and thus disguised) when vertical strips are placed side by side. In each of the drawings below, rotation produces a continuous design, but a drop pattern is only possible with the right-hand one. Can you see why?

A selection of early tiles from Turkey and England which show the staggering complexity of design which can arise from the simple acts of rotation and translation of a unit.

BLOCK PRINTED REPEATS
thinking outside the box

Production methods often affect design. In printing, for example, although hand-carved wooden blocks of many shapes (e.g. rhombs or hexagons) are sometimes used, finished designs are most often rationalized into rectangles. This makes them easier to transfer onto rollers and facilitates the simple alignment of edges and corners as the inks are finally pressed onto the fabric or paper.

To help create designs that flow organically beyond such artificial limits, a designer can reconfigure a rectangle, removing corners and redistributing them to create a shape which also tessellates and has the same area as the original rectangle. This technique has the virtue of allowing the artist to respond to a new shape and see new possibilities (*see below*).

A "turnover" is a design which uses reflection to generate a wider pattern. In many turnover designs, details along the central axis are deliberately asymmetrical to create visual interest.

This page: Four 19th-century designs by William Morris, exhibiting a mastery of composition and color. Above: A drop repeat. Below: Turnover design with underlying left-right symmetry disguised by asymmetry in the leafy detail. Top right: Spiral vines and a scattering of flowers make up a design with no obvious structure. Below right: Alternating boughs move in and out of the governing rectangle.

COMPOSITIONAL TECHNIQUES
inside the boxes

Whilst block printing helps the designer plan at large scales, additional techniques assist with the creation of a pattern.

When setting out a design, the area to be filled is often divided into a grid with certain boxes selected for emphasis. This strategy allows for the planning of open spaces or large motifs as well as the distribution of color effects (particularly useful when the designer wishes to minimize unwanted linear effects).

Several useful 19th-century tricks are shown here. Below, a 6×6 grid is used to organize a scattering of leaves, to beautiful effect. Because only one square in each row or column is selected, the appearance of stripes is cleverly avoided. In the upper diagrams opposite, a similar grid system structures the placement of large motifs and open spaces.

It is impossible to demonstrate here the effects of color, but it is worth remembering that, like so many things in nature, colors have opposites and friends, and two colors with the same gray value placed side by side can confuse the eye. Using only color, a repeated unit can create a pattern all by itself (*opposite lower right*).

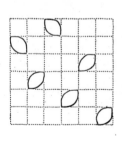 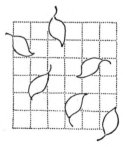 

The flowers in this square block have been distributed using a 6×6 grid system. Notice how the flowers have been tilted in 6 different directions.

In this leafy composition, particular boxes in the 5×5 block were determined in advance to create a balanced set of spaces within the overall design.

Diamond units are the basis for this design, but by combining them as strips in a long zigzag, interesting new possibilities become available.

Color introduces further variation and complexity into a design. New subtle lines and stripes can appear which may or may not be intentional.

Proving a Pattern
refining the design

It is vital to thoroughly test the basic unit of any new repeat pattern to ensure that when printed, no unexpected effects will emerge. For example, in the drop pattern below, no matter which corners or edges are joined, positive and negative areas remain balanced and all motifs are completed. To be confident about the final effect it is advisable to repeat the design several times. This allows the designer to see stripes or lines that might unintentionally emerge, or to strengthen motifs that may recede in visual strength when repeated in a pattern.

The example opposite shows how a design can extend beyond the limits of the printing block. Motifs that burst outside the frame on one side can be found creeping in on the opposite edge.

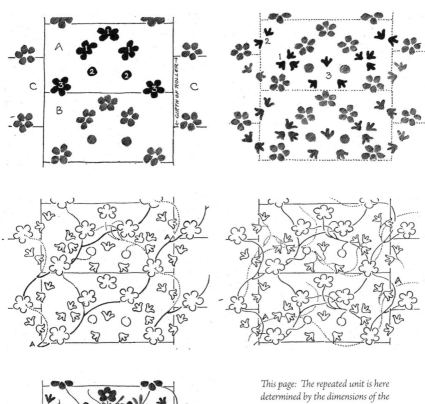

This page: The repeated unit is here determined by the dimensions of the printer's roller. The pattern is designed with a drop repeat and the designer's sketch extends beyond the boundaries of the roller's rectangle to better predict how the design will look when repeated. Details are added after the lines and masses are established. In this example, the flowers were symmetrically arranged to establish a visual rhythm, but are connected by slanting vines which twine asymmetrically through the open spaces.

TURNING A CORNER
bringing it all together

There are a number of different ways to turn a corner. In the medieval illuminated French manuscript borders below, a leafed vine design has been organically adapted to move around a corner, demonstrating how to build up a skeleton of curves populated with foliate elements using no repetition or reflection. This approach works well in a unique hand-painted design, but is obviously less suited to block printing.

When creating a system of units that can be slid, rotated, or reflected, corners must be considered carefully. A 45° mitred corner can require the enlarging or stretching of the border design, or even the composition of something entirely new. Sometimes, the designer may simply "box off" the corner to avoid such labor.

With the inclusion of lengthening pieces and turnover units (*opposite lower right*), a basic square motif can be adapted to a variety of purposes by making it longer or wider. In the example shown, there are five unique units that constitute the central composition. These standard units have then been rotated and reflected as necessary to create the much larger composition.

Above left: Corner detail from Sultan Beybar's 1304 Quran, with corner section derived from the edge border units. Above right: A border which is a continuous part of the central design.

Above: Strategies for planning a bordered textile composition using turnovers and lengthening pieces. With this flexible approach, designs can be adapted to be as large or as small as necessary.

CONSTRUCTED CURVES
tracery, volutes, and moldings

Architects often soften their structures with curves in the form of arched windows, doorways, or other features. These are drawn with compasses from multiple centers (*e.g. below, trefoil and quatrefoil windows, arches, ellipses, and ovals*). Similarly, subtly moving the center allows an Ionic volute to be drawn using compasses and ruler (*opposite top left*). Wooden or plastic "French" or "Burmester" curves (*opposite top right*) are useful templates which allow a designer to find a portion of a required curve between two points.

Moldings in plaster, wood, or stone are decorative features perceived as straight lines of light and shadow. When viewed in profile they can reveal unexpected sophistication (*lower opposite*).

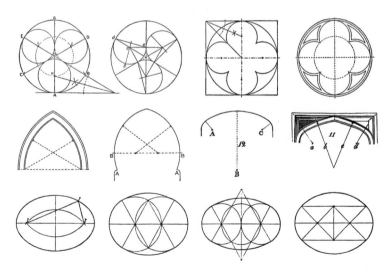

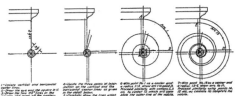

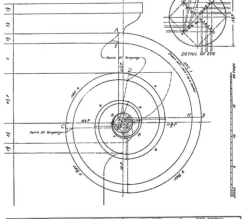

DETAIL OF EYE

Left: The Ionic Volute by Wooster Bard Field, 1920. Above: French curves and garment rulers, very useful for drawing curves. Below: Moldings soften corners.

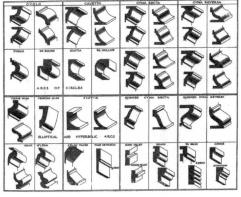

41

ARCHES AND DOMES
leafy forests of stone

Biomorphic ornamentation is not just limited to the plane. In the same way that flowing branches emerge from the confines of two-dimensional grids, structural arches and domes awaken the tedious cubes and straight lines of three-dimensional architectural spaces into forms more resembling those of living things.

The largest plants are trees, and it is the powerful form of the tree that is most evident in columns, arches, and fan vaulting (*opposite top right*). Leaf-like tracery suggests the play of branches, and colorful rose windows shine like flowers in a dark forest. Passing through a tall arch is similar to walking through a grove of trees, their magnificent branches vaulting overhead.

Domes, the quintessential symbol of heavenly perfection, are a curve spun around a central axis, and suggest emergent buds, shoots, or breasts, bursting full with the promise of life. They can be pointed, hemispherical, segmented, or onion, and are often covered, inside and outside, with cosmological ornamentation.

Above left: Arches constructed of interlocking circles and curves. Above right: English cathedral fan vaulting, echoing the branches of a forest arbor. Below: Decorated arches from a palace in Tanjore, India. Opposite page: Pointed Mamluk domes from Cairo.

THE ART OF THE BOOK
illuminating the word

Ornamentation has long been used to supplement a sacred text, such as the Bible or Quran. This labor-intensive and time-consuming process takes great skill. Frequently, the decoration responds to the written word, as gold and bright pigments reflect the physical light as a fitting complement to the spiritual illumination of the sacred writings. Sometimes this may take the form of an illustrated scene described in the text; in other cases the connection is more abstract.

By far the most frequent ornamentation is plant-based, with foliates and flowers climbing the margins, marking the beginnings of chapter and verse, or carpeting a double frontispiece in a lavish paradise garden of golden vines, leaves, and blossoms.

Book decoration enjoyed a resurgence during the 19th-century British Arts and Crafts movement (*see examples below*), often with a similar symbolic correlation between text and ornament.

  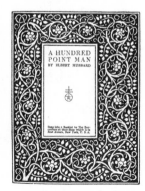

Left: Detail from a carpet page illumination in an 11th-century Persian Quran. Within the lovely 8-fold rosette, doubled spiralling branches perfectly fill the available space. Beyond the medallion, the spiral is complemented by curving clouds.

Below: Detail from an illuminated page in the 7th-century Lindisfarne gospels, a beautiful repository of Celtic Christian Art. Here the Greek letters chi and rho are decorated with intricate spirals, a veritable symphony of swirls.

PEN AND BRUSH
penmanship and flourishes

The art of pen or brush is perhaps the most ubiquitous form of curvilinear expression, available to everyone who has ever hand-written a note. It is an art form that emerges from the rhythms of the body, an internal state of mind revealed in curves, loops, and flourishes. It is possible that "handwriting, being a manifestation of one who writes, somehow reproduces something of its writer's temperament, personality, or character" (Camillo Baldi, 1621).

Clarity and fluidity, highly prized by artists and designers, can be refined by a careful study of the calligraphic arts. These demand both precision and spontaneity, regulation and rule-breaking, directness and circuitousness (*e.g. see flourishes by Ann Hechle, opposite*). Whether produced with a reed, steel nib, or brush as in the Norwegian acanthus rosmaling design below (note the seed principle, flowers in plan and elevation, and the teardrop-shaped brush strokes), the quality of line in a calligraphic composition can be a thing of beauty.

flourishing

flourishing

flourishing

MARBLED PAPERS
dynamically fluid

Marbled paper provides an opportunity to see curved patterns of ebb and flow that normally are too transient to observe closely when in liquid form. The subtle chaos, captured as a one-time monotype on paper (or sometimes silk), is a microcosmic echo of the tides and currents, whirlwinds, and tsunamis, which have been induced by the artist. Ripples, vortices, striations, flourishes, and turbulences are all captured, frozen in time. Unlike most other decorative ornamentation, in marbling there is no difference between positive and negative space.

To marble, very finely ground color oil pigments or inks are floated on the surface of water or a viscous solution. Various additives prevent the colors and solutions from mixing. The artist carefully manipulates the design using breath, brushes, feathers, or special combs, before a single sheet of paper or silk, quickly applied to the surface, receives the unique imprint of the composition.

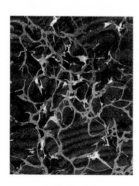  

PAISLEY
pregnant with possibility

The "paisley" shape takes its name from the Scottish town which produced patterned shawls inspired by Kashmiri textiles in the 19th century. Incredibly elastic, the *boteh* can become short and squat, lean and elongated, or everything in between. It is variously thought to represent a mango, the new shoot of a date palm, a tadpole or fish, a pine tree, or the human form.

Like its close cousin the yin-yang, the *boteh* is full of paradox. It is both watery and flamelike, simultaneously a single leaf and the archetypal tree of life, a body curled into a fetal position swelling with life and potential, and the infinite abundance of paradise reflected in a single drop of water.

THE TREE OF LIFE
and gardens of paradise

A cosmic tree is revered in some form in virtually every culture. It manifests variously as olive, date, fig, pomegranate, fir, almond, bo, oak, yew, mulberry, maize, or bamboo.

The essence of this archetypal tree is implicit within biomorphic decorations as both a visual pattern and a mythological matrix—its roots draw nourishment from the darkness of the earth, its trunk stretches upward against the pull of gravity, and its branches spiral across the heavens to leaf, flower, and bear fruit.

Nature's beauty and ingenuity perpetually inspire and direct human creativity. Echoes of her order and abundant variety are manifest in ornamentation and loved by her entire human family.

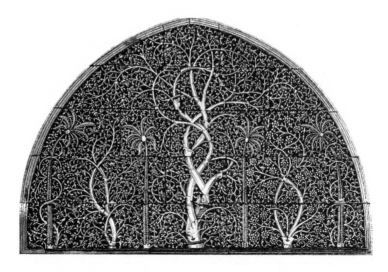

Top left: *Gold oak leaf crown, Macedonia, 350 BC.* Top right: *Gold myrtle wreath, Greece, 150 BC.*
Above: *Traditional Sarawak painted world tree, Borneo.* Opposite: *Stone screen, Ahmedabad, India.*
Below left: *Detailed biomorphic woodcarving, Malaysia.* Below right: *Carved wooden doors, Thailand.*

APPENDIX I ~ MATHEMATICAL CURVES

Many of the common two- and three-dimensional mathematical curves are shown here.
Bezier curves are today widely used to produce smooth curves in computer applications.

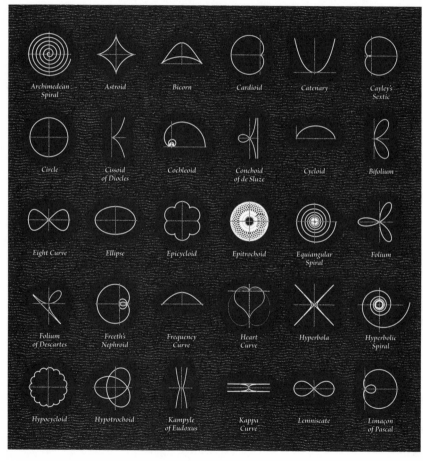

Lissajous
Curve

Lituus
Spiral

Logarithmic
Spiral

Neil's
Parabola

Nephroid

Parabola

Parabolic
Spiral

Plateau
Curve

Rhodonea
Curve 1

Rhodonea
Curve 2

Right
Strophoid

Serpentine

Spiral of
Archimedes

Talbot's
Curve

Tractrix

Tricuspoid

Trifolium

Witch of
Agnesi

Quadratic
Bezier Curve

Cubic
Bezier Curve

Cubic
Bezier Curve

Cubic
Bezier Curve

Cubic
Bezier Curve

Quartic
Bezier Curve

Circular
Helix

Conical
Helix

Cylindrical
Sine

Spheroidal
Sine

Hyperboloidal
Sine

Conical
Sine

Viviani's
Curve

Sici
Spiral

Fresnel
Spiral

Toroidal
Spiral

Spherical
Spiral

Rotating
Sine

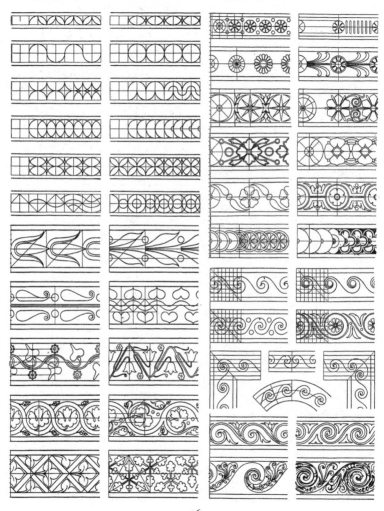

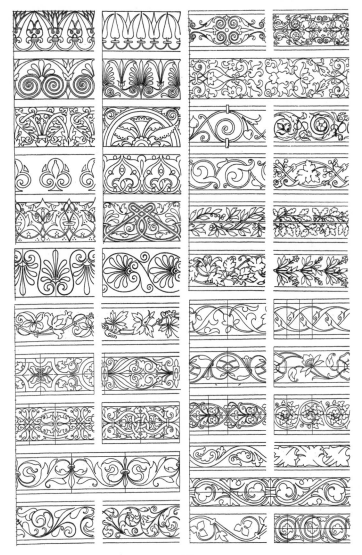

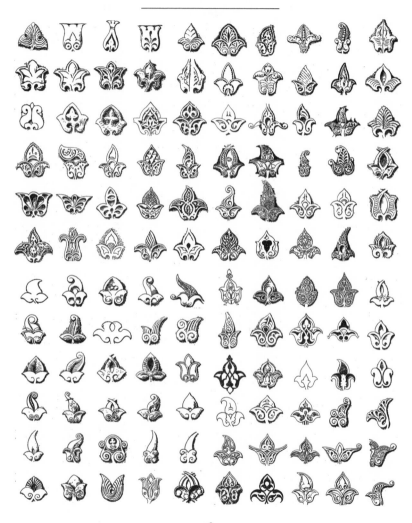